ALEXANDER GELMAN

A MAN WITH CONNECTIONS

Translated by Stephen Mulrine

A Royal Court Programme /Text published by
NICK HERN BOOKS
A division of Walker Books Limited

This edition of *A Man with Connections*, containing the text as adapted for performance at the Traverse and Royal Court Theatres, was first published in 1989 as an original paperback by Nick Hern Books, a division of Walker Books Limited, 87 Vauxhall Walk, London SE11 5HJ. The full text is printed in *Stars in the Morning Sky*, an anthology of new Soviet plays edited by Michael Glenny, also published by Nick Hern Books.

Set in Baskerville
by Book Ens, Saffron Walden, Essex
Printed by Expression Printers Limited, London N7 9DP

British Library Cataloguing in Publication Data

Gelman, Alexander
    A man with connections
    1. Drama in Russia 1945–English texts
    I. Title
    891.72'44
    ISBN 1 85459 006 5

COMING NEXT

IN THE MAIN HOUSE   730 1745

23 February — 25 March

MY MOTHER SAID I NEVER SHOULD

by Charlotte Keatley. Directed by Michael Attenborough
Set designed by Robin Don. Costumes designed by Jennifer Cook

Charlotte Keatley's warm, funny and engrossing play has its London
premiere at the Royal Court. Shifting gently back and forth in time, it
contrasts the loves and expectations of four generations of women and
builds a poignant and human picture of the richness of family life from
the beginning of this century.
Winner of the 1987 George Devine Award.

SUNDAYS 26 February, 5, 12, 19 March

DAGMAR KRAUSE
SINGS WORKS BY HANNS EISLER

Dagmar Krause is the finest contemporary interpreter of the German song
tradition. Her latest work, devoted to the songs of Hanns Eisler, will be
unveiled at this series of concerts.

15, 16, 17 March

THREE ARTS MANAGEMENT SEMINARS

A series of seminars have been arranged, aimed at school and college
leavers, as an introduction to the field of arts management.

IN THE THEATRE UPSTAIRS   730 2554

12-28 January

The Royal Court Young People's Theatre present

A ROCK IN WATER

by Winsome Pinnock. Directed by Elyse Dodgson
A play inspired by the life of Claudia Jones

A ROCK IN WATER tells the largely unknown story of Claudia Jones, one of
the great black community leaders of our time. It charts her fascinating
life from Trinidad to Harlem and her persecution and trial for 'Un-
American Activities', to her enforced exile in England, where she founded
the West Indian Gazette and initiated the first now legendary, Caribbean
Carnival.

16 February — 11 March

The Womens Playhouse Trust in association with
the Royal Court Theatre present

A HERO'S WELCOME

by Winsome Pinnock
Directed by Jules Wright. Designed by Lucy Weller

A HERO'S WELCOME is a play about a small community. It follows the
stories of three young women, Minda, Sis and Ishbel, growing up in the
Caribbean in 1947, and the men who seem to offer a way out — Len, the
hero of the title, and Stanley an insidious charmer. Their imaginings are
checked by the realism of older women, Nana and Mrs Walker. This richly
textured, erotic play in which tragedy and politics are placed in a precise
context and the delicate humour and density of Winsome Pinnocks
writing emerges with exceptional strength.

THE PATRONAGE SCHEME
AT THE ROYAL COURT

For many years now Members of the Royal Court Theatre Society have received special notice of new productions, but why not become a **Friend, Associate** or a **Patron of the Royal Court**, thereby involving yourself directly in maintaining the high standard and unique quality of Royal Court productions — while enjoying complimentary tickets to the shows themselves?

1 MEMBERSHIP SCHEME

For £10 you will receive details of all forthcoming events via the Royal Court *Member's Letter,* and be entitled to purchase any available seat for £3 during previews (maximum of two per Member).

2 FRIENDS OF THE ROYAL COURT

For £35 (or £50 joint membership) you will be entitled to one (or two) complimentary preview ticket(s) for performances on the Main Stage and one (or two) preview tickets for productions in the Theatre Upstairs. You will automatically be on our mailing list and be invited to all lectures and special events.

3 ASSOCIATES OF THE ROYAL COURT

For £350 you will be entitled to four top price tickets (previews or press nights) to all Main House productions and four tickets to all plays in the Theatre Upstairs.

4 MEMBERSHIP SCHEME

For £1,000 you can make a 'personal appearance' on a plaque in the Royal Court lobby, and appear in our programme. In addition, you will be entitled to six free tickets for shows in the Main House or the Theatre Upstairs.

When you have chosen from the four categories, please make your cheque/P.O. payable to the *Royal Court Theatre Society* and send to: *Max Stafford-Clark, Artistic Director, Royal Court Theatre, Sloane Square, London SW1.* Alternatively, if you wish to covenant for four years or more by filling in the form which you will find in the theatre foyer, we — as a registered charity — can claim back the tax you have already paid, thereby increasing the value of your donation.

PATRONS

Caryl Churchill, Alfred Davis, Mrs. Henny Gestetner, Lady Eileen Joseph, Henry Kaye, Richard King, Tracey Ullman, Julian Wadham.

ASSOCIATES

Richard Barran, Peter Boizot, David Capelli, Michael Codron, Stephen Fry, Elizabeth Garvie, The Earl of Gowrie, Patricia Marmont, Barbara Minto, David Mirvish, Greville Poke, Michael Serlin, Sir Dermot de Trafford, Nick Hern Books, Richard Wilson.

FRIENDS

Paul Adams, Robin Anderson, Jane Anhakin, John Arthur, Mrs. M. Baghust, Linda Bassett, Paul Bater, Josephine Beddoe, Bob Boas, Katie Bradford, Jim Broadbent, Alan Brodie, A.J.H. Buckley, Guy Chapman, Angela Coles, Miss C. Collingwood, Jeremy Conway, Lou Coulson, Peter Cregeen, Alan David, Mrs. Der Pao Graham, Anne Devlin, Ann Diamond, Mrs. V.A. Dimant, R.H. & B.H. Dowler, Adrian Charles Dunbar, Susan Dunnett, Pamela Edwardes, George A. Elliott III, Jan Evans, Trevor Eve, Kenneth Ewing, Kate Feast, Gilly Fraser, David Gant, Kerry Gardner, Anne Garwood, Jonathan Gems, Lord Goodman, Rod Hall, Sharon Hamper, Jan Harvey, Sarah Hellings, Jocelyn Herbert, Davild Horovitch, Dusty Hughes, Kenny Ireland, Alison E. Jackson, Richard Jackson, Dick Jarrett, Hugh Jenkins, Dominic Jephcott, Paul Jesson, Elizabeth Karr Tashman, Sharon Kean, Alice Kennelly, Sir Kerry & Lady St. Johnston, Mrs. O. Lahr, Dr. R.J. Lande, Iain Lanyon, Hugh Laurie, Alison Leathart, Sheila Lemon, Roger & Moira Lubbock, John & Erica Macdonald, Suzie Mackenzie, Barbara Mackie, Marina Martin, Anna Massey, Paul Matthews, Philip L. McDonald, Ian McMillan, James Midgley, Louise Miller, Anthony Mingella, Sally Newton, John Nicholls, Nick Marston, Richard O'Brien, Eileen & John O'Keefe, Donal O'Leary, Stephen Oliver, Gary Olsen, Norma Papp, Ronald Pickup, Pauline Pinder, Harold Pinter, Peter Polkinghorne, Margaret Ramsay, Jane Rayne, Alan Rickman, Dr. P.A. Rixon, David Robb, Rosemary Squire, A.J. Sayers, Leah Schmidt, Jennifer Sebag-Montefiore, Mrs. L.M. Sieff, Paul Sinclair Brooks, Jane Snowden, Louise Stein, Jeff Steitzer, Lindsay Stevens, Pearl Stewart, Richard Stokes, Richard Stone, Rob Sutherland, Dudley Sutton, Audrey & Gordon Taylor, Steve Tedbury, Nigel Terry, Mary Trevelyan, Mrs. Anne Underwood, Maureen Vincent, Andrew Wadsworth, Harriet Walter, Julie Walters, Julia M. Walters, Sarah Wheatland, Charles & Victoria Wright.

FOR THE ROYAL COURT

DIRECTION

Artistic Director.. MAX STAFFORD-CLARK
Deputy Director .... SIMON CURTIS
Casting Director..LISA MAKIN
Literary Manager ....KATE HARWOOD
Assistant Director   PHILIP HOWARD
Artistic Assistant .... MELANIE KENYON

PRODUCTION

Production Manager ....BO BARTON
Technical Manager, Theatre Upstairs ....CHRIS BAGUST
Chief Electrician ....COLIN ROXBOROUGH
Deputy Chief Electrician ....MARK BRADLEY
Electrician .... DENIS O'HARE*
Sound Designer.. BRYAN BOWEN
Acting Master Carpenter...JOHN BURGESS
Acting Deputy Carpenter..MATTHEW SMITH
Wardrobe Supervisor ....JENNIFER COOK
Deputy Wardrobe Supervisor....................................CATHIE SKILBECK

ADMINISTRATION

General Manager...GRAHAM COWLEY
Assistant to General Manager.................................... LUCY WOOLLATT
Finance Administrator...STEPHEN MORRIS
Finance Assistant ....GILL RUSSELL
Press Manager .... SALLY LYCETT
Marketing & Publicity Manager .... GUY CHAPMAN
Development Director...TOM PETZAL
Development Assistant .... JACQUELINE VIEIRA
House Manager..WILLIAM DAY
Deputy House Manager ....ALISON SMITH
Box Office Manager.. STEVEN CURRIE
Box Office Assistants.................................... GERALD BROOKING, ROSALEEN DEW
Box Office Trainee ....RITA SHARMA*
Stage Door/Telephonists .... ANGELA TOULMIN, CERI SHIELDS*
Evening Stage Door ....TYRONE LUCAS*
Maintenance...JOHN LORRIGIO*
Cleaners...EILEEN CHAPMAN*, IVY JONES*
Firemen .... MARK BRYERS*, PAUL KLEINMANN*

YOUNG PEOPLE'S THEATRE

Director ....ELYSE DODGSON
Temporary Administrator ....DOMINIC TICKELL
*Part-time staff

COUNCIL: Chairman: MATTHEW EVANS, CHRIS BAGUST, BO BARTON, STUART BURGE,
ANTHONY C. BURTON, CARYL CHURCHILL, BRIAN COX, HARRIET CRUICKSHANK, SIMON
CURTIS, ALLAN DAVIS, DAVID LLOYD DAVIS, ROBERT FOX, MRS. HENNY GESTETNER OBE,
DEREK GRANGER, DAVID HARE, JOCELYN HERBERT, DAVID KLEEMAN, HANIF KUREISHI,
SONIA MELCHETT, JAMES MIDGLEY, JOAN PLOWRIGHT CBE, GREVILLE POKE, JANE RAYNE,
JIM TANNER, SIR HUGH WILLIATT.

This Theatre is associated with the Thames Television Playwright Scheme, and the
Regional Theatre Young Directors Scheme.

PHOTOS OF A MAN WITH CONNECTIONS
by Sean Hudson

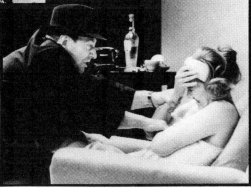

A MAN WITH CONNECTIONS
BY ALEXANDER GELMAN
Translated by Stephen Mulrine

NATASHA GLADKOV...........................Marty Cruickshank
ANDREI GLADKOV...Bill Paterson

Voice of Alyosha Gladkov...........................Simon Donald

Directed by...Jenny Killick
Designed by.. Dermot Hayes

Lighting and Sound....................................George Tarbuck
Company Stage Manager .... Jacqui Jeffrey
Deputy Stage Manager ....Lucy Conway
Assistant Stage Manager ....Sarah Jay
Production Photographs................................Sean Hudson
Poster design.. Simon Williams
Leaflet design ....Sightlines

Set and costumes made in
the Traverse Workshop and Wardrobe

THERE WILL BE NO INTERVAL

The British Premiere of A MAN WITH CONNECTIONS was at the
Traverse Theatre, Edinburgh, on 4 August 1988

Wardrobe care by PERSIL and BIO-TEX. Adhesive by COPYDEX and EVODE LTD. Ioniser for the
lighting control room by THE LONDON IONISER CENTRE (836 0211). Cordless drill by MAKITA
ELECTRIC (UK) LTD. Watches by THE TIMEX CORPORATION. Batteries by EVER READY,
refrigerators by ELECTROLUX and PHILLIPS MAJOR APPLIANCES LTD. Microwaves by TOSHIBA
UK LTD. Kettles for rehearsals by MORPHY RICHARDS. Television for backstage by GRANADA.
Video for casting purposes by HITACHI. Cold bottled beers at the bar supplied by YOUNG &
CO. BREWERY, WANDSWORTH. Coffee machines by CONA.

FOR THE TRAVERSE:

Funded by

FINANCIALLY ASSISTED BY THE
ROYAL BOROUGH OF
KENSINGTON AND CHELSEA

BIOGRAPHIES

MARTY CRUICKSHANK For the Royal Court:
BACKBONE and author/editor of ROYAL BOROUGH. Other theatre
includes: seasons at the Glasgow Citizens, Oxford Playhouse and
Bristol Old Vic, SLAG and FANSHEN (Hampstead), THE END OF ME
OLD CIGAR (Greenwich), TWELFTH NIGHT (Young Vic), STRAIGHT UP
(Piccadilly), ABSURD PERSON SINGULAR (Criterion), THE WORLD
TURNED UPSIDE DOWN and A FAIR QUARREL (National), THE HOUSE
(Joint Stock), BURIED CHILD (Hampstead), EARLY DAYS (Comedy),
IN THE MOOD (Hampstead), NUMBER OF THE BEAST (Bush), GREAT
AND SMALL (Vaudeville), THE CHERRY ORCHARD (Leicester
Haymarket), EXTREMITIES (Duchess), BEAUTY AND THE BEAST
(Liverpool Playhouse and Old Vic), THE SEAGULL (Liverpool
Playhouse), CURTAINS (Whitehall). Recent television includes
GOOD BEHAVIOUR (BBC), STUDIO (Granada), CHARLIE (Central),
FRANKIE AND JOHNNIE (BBC). Films include CLOSING RANKS.
Writing credits; THE PRINCESS OF CLEVES (performed at the ICA)
and, currently working on a new translation of BEATRICE AND
BENEDICT for the English National Opera.

DERMOT HAYES Most recent design for the Royal
Court: THE LAST SUPPER. Other recent work includes SUMMER
AND SMOKE (Leicester Haymarket), YERMA (Abbey Theatre),
OBSERVE THE SONS OF ULSTER MARCHING TOWARDS THE SOMME
(Hampstead), HEDDA GABLER (Rogoland Theatre, Norway),
TWELFTH NIGHT (Leicester Haymarket), A MAN WITH CONNECTIONS
(Traverse).

JENNY KILLICK Artistic Director of Traverse Theatre
(1983–1988). Credits include THROUGH THE LEAVES, NOAH'S WIFE,
CORA, LUCY'S PLAY, LOSING VENICE, PLAYING WITH FIRE and A MAN
WITH CONNECTIONS.

BILL PATERSON Founder member of 7:84 (Scotland).
Productions include THE CHEVIOT, THE STAG and THE BLACK,
BLACK OIL, WHOSE LIFE IS IT ANYWAY? (Savoy), ELLA (ICA), GUYS
AND DOLLS and SCHWEYK IN THE SECOND WORLD WAR (National),
CRIME AND PUNISHMENT (Lyric Hammersmith). Television includes
LICKING HITLER, THE VANISHING ARMY, SMILEY'S PEOPLE,
AUFWIEDERSEHN PET, THE SINGING DETECTIVE and THE
INTERROGATION OF JOHN. Films include THE KILLING FIELDS,
COMFORT AND JOY, A PRIVATE FUNCTION, DEFENCE OF THE REALM
FRIENDSHIP'S DEATH.

GEORGE TARBUCK Has worked extensively in both
Britain and Europe as Stage Manager, Lighting Director, special
effect and explosives consultant. He is resident Lighting Designer
at the Traverse and has lit the majority of the Traverse shows
during the last five years.

ALEXANDER GELMAN

Alexander Isaakovich Gelman (b.1933) is one of the Soviet Union's foremost modern playwrights. His work includes **PROTOKOL ODNOGO ZASEDANIYA** (MINUTES OF A MEETING 1976), **MY,NIZHE PODPISAVSHIESYA** (WE, THE UNDERSIGNED 1979) and **NAEDINE SO VSEMI** (A MAN WITH CONNECTIONS 1982). A graduate of Kishinev University, and a Party member since 1956, Gelman worked as a machine operator and a builder before becoming a journalist in 1967. Since the early 1970s his output has expanded to include film and TV scripts, as well as the stage plays on which his fame chiefly rests. His best-known plays belong to the popular Soviet genre of 'Workplace Drama', and he frequently explores the theme of conflict between career and family life, ethics and success. A personal friend of Mikhail Gorbachov, Gelman was proposed by the Premier as a delegate at the recent Communist Party Conference. The proposal was rejected by the Moscow Communist Party.

Photo Chris Hill

Photo Sean Hudson

JENNY KILLICK

Photo Sean Hudson

Tilda Swinton in Manfred Karge's
MAN TO MAN.

ABOUT THE TRAVERSE

Simon Donald and Tom Mannion in
Simon Donald's PRICKLY HEAT

Edinburgh's tiny 100 seat theatre — the first studio theatre in the world — has this year been celebrating an improbable anniversary. The Traverse opened, 25 years ago, in a former brothel off the Royal Mile, where a handful of subscribers gathered on a bitterly cold night in January 1963 to watch the opening production— Sartre's *Huis Clos*. On the second night, the accidental on-stage stabbing of the leading actress propelled the fledgling theatre club into the headlines, where, by one means or another, it has since remained.

Born out of the euphoria of the early Edinburgh Fringe — and the Quixotic vision of a small group of committed individuals — the Theatre has survived, against all the odds, to become the only Theatre outside London entirely dedicated to the production of new British and international work. In the last quarter century it has launched the careers of some of our best-known writers, actors, directors and designers.

In the words of the critic, Michael Billington, the Traverse has "profoundly affected both the architecture and the ethos of modern theatre. Exactly like the Royal Court, the Traverse has an influence on our culture totally out of proportion to its size or its subsidy. The health of our television, film and theatre stems from the obstinate faith in writers shown by companies like the Traverse . . . "

The roll-call of writers whose first, or early works, were seen at the Traverse reads like a Who's Who of British theatre: Howard Barker, Peter Barnes, Steven Berkoff, Howard Brenton, John Byrne, David Edgar, Marcella Evaristi, Trevor Griffiths, David Hare, Robert Holman, Liz Lochhead, Claire Luckham, Tom McGrath, Mustapha Matura, Mike Stott, C.P. Taylor, Michael Wilcox and Heathcote Williams.

Alexander Gelman's *A Man with Connections* is only the most recent in a long line of important international works premiered at the Traverse. The Theatre has given British premieres to plays by Bertolt Brecht, Saul Bellow, Marguerite Duras, Max Frisch, Gunter Grass, Franz Xavier Kroetz, Yukio Mishima, Sam Shepard, Barney Simon, Michael Tremblay and Mario Vargas Llosa.

Over the years Traverse productions have transferred to theatres all over the world. The Royal Court itself set the trend in 1964 by taking Michael Geliot's spectacularly successful production of Brecht's *Happy End* — starring opera singer Bettina Jonic and with sets designed by the young Ralph Koltai and Nadine Bayliss.

Since then the Royal Court has welcomed a steady stream of Traverse productions — and one former Artistic Director in the shape of Max Stafford-Clark.

In 1978, with the transfer of *The Slab Boys*, Royal Court audiences were the first outside Scotland to witness the extraordinary talents of the Glasgow writer/artist John Byrne — whose *Tutti Frutti* has been the undisputed highlight of recent television drama. In January, Tilda Swinton's stunning solo performance of Manfred Karge's *Man to Man* was hailed by The Listener as 'one of the theatrical feats of a turbulent decade'.

The driving force behind the Traverse has always been that of change. The Theatre has been through many different incarnations in the 25 years since 1963 and, as the Traverse nears the end of its Silver Jubilee year, it is preparing to reinvent itself once again, with the departure of Jenny Killick and the appointment of Ian Brown as Artistic Director.

In 3 years time the Theatre will take its boldest step since the move from former brothel to former sailmaker's loft in 1969 — by taking up residence in a brand-new space on the site of Edinburgh's notorious Hole-in-the-Ground. The New Traverse will be the first new theatre built in Edinburgh this century and the first purpose-built new writing theatre ever in Britain.

ALEXANDER GELMAN AND THE 'GORBACHOV REVOLUTION' IN SOVIET THEATRE
by Michael Glenny

Mikhail Gorbachov's relaxation of censorship and of control over the arts in the USSR has had its most immediate and vitalising effect in the Soviet theatre. This has begun to arouse in Britain a wholly new interest in Russian plays, as listeners to Radio 3, watchers of 'The South Bank Show', Edinburgh Festival goers and other connoisseurs of interesting theatrical marginalia may have noticed. The present production of Alexander Gelman's *A Man with Connections* represents a considerable advance in the recognition of modern Soviet drama in Britain — a step forward from the airwaves and the festivals towards the West End; there are, after all, enough precedents for Sloane Square being a stepping-stone to Shaftesbury Avenue.

London, though has a poor record when it comes to importing straight plays from abroad; when did you last see a French, German or Italian play, in the West End? And modern Russian plays — anything post-Chekhov — are rarer still. This is partly due to our general theatrical xenophobia (despite such honourable exceptions as the revived Old Vic), but chiefly it is because all Soviet plays have been automatically dismissed as little else but heavy-handed propaganda, not merely hopelessly uncommercial but uninteresting even for the supposedly questing, experimental Fringe.

In the pre-Gorbachov era there was admittedly some truth in this, although when under the late unlamented Brezhnev a handful of good plays did manage to get staged in the Soviet Union, they never reached these shores. Generally speaking, as long as the official doctrine of 'Socialist Realism' was in force, as it was until recently, Soviet playwrights were under pressure to show audiences a picture of their own society summed up in a formula that ran something like this: 'Eat up your nice bread-and-butter today, and if we all do as nanny tells us there will be jam tomorrow'.

Glasnost, which began to hit Soviet theatres in 1986, has transformed the Soviet stage by the virtual abolition of censorship and the removal of the dead hand of the Ministry of Culture from the choice of repertoire. The process was greatly helped by Vladimir Gubaryev's play *Sarcophagus*, a piece of urgent dramatic journalism about the Chernobyl disaster which, like the event that inspired it, blew the lid off any attempts to suppress it. 'Socialist Realism' has been consigned to Trotsky's famous "dustbin of history". Official propaganda is out; conventional 'heroes' have gone; sane scepticism has become the author's standpoint; and moral ambiguity replaces dogmatic certainty, the resulting plays are infinitely more realistic, moving and truthful than the contrived situations and inauthentic, schematised characterisation which made too many Soviet plays into mere political lantern-lectures — the sort of plays, in fact, which were steadily emptying Soviet theatres in the 1970's and early 1980's

By contrast, *A Man with Connections* is one of the new wave of plays which have been bringing capacity audiences back into those theatres. Some of this turn-around has been achieved by importing such brilliant comedies as Michael Frayn's *Noises Off*, playing to full houses in Moscow, in a wonderfully ingenious Russian translation. Equally, Soviet playwrights have suddenly been able to write about social reality as *they* see it and not in accordance with dogma and ideology. In this play, Alexander Gelman makes a telling frontal assault on a part of the Soviet system which, as Gelman sees it, breeds hypocrisy, cheating and double standards and corrupts the personality of anyone professionally obliged to try and make the system work. This and other new plays, different though they may be in form and subject-matter, are part of an upsurge of new writing for the stage which in the Soviet context is revolutionary. As well as bearing the inimitable stamp of credibility that is the mark of writing based on an author's experience and convictions, they have also, at a stroke, overturned the deadening formulae inherited from Stalin: instead of the individual being the villain who is betraying the system and preventing it from functioning properly, it is the appallingly flawed system itself that is shown up as the force crushing and dehumanising the individual.

Born in 1939, Alexander Gelman is one of today's most performed playwrights in the Soviet Union. Several of his earlier plays were located in factories and other workplaces. They managed to pass the now abolished theatre censorship and get performed because they outwardly corresponded in type to an officially approved genre: the 'production drama', in which a group of honest workers, usually spearheaded by a keen young (or wise old) Party member, succeed in 'unmasking' an inefficient or corrupt manager and having him ousted in the final scene. Gelman's plays in this mode were, however, deceptive: not being built around simplistic Communist Party slogans but on plausibly real clashes of personality, they were psychologically authentic and at the same time subversive of stereotyped, dogmatic attitudes.

A Man with Connections also concerns a senior manager in Soviet industry who is in trouble, in this case a departmental head in a civil engineering and construction enterprise, but there any resemblance to the cliche-ridden 'production dramas' of the past stops. This play, in fact, could have been consciously written as a grim, upside-down parody of that discredited genre: most importantly, the action takes place between a man and his wife in their own home and not in the usual public arena such as the boardroom, the factory floor or a building site; here there is no chorus of honest, indignant workers; no *deus ex machina* from the Party or the ministry descends in the last act to dispense justice and put everything to rights. The play is much more of a tragedy in the classic sense of a man destroyed by his very qualities — or what pass for qualities in the creaking, inefficient, often corrupt world of Soviet industry. It is also a truly classic piece in that it observes the Aristotelian unities of time, place and action, while the only departure from the two-character dialogue are a few brief but heart-stopping lines from a voice on the telephone — the modern equivalent of the Messenger in ancient Greek tragedy.

While our theatre managers love two-handers because they are cheap to produce, they are relatively rare in Soviet playwriting. In the USSR — a country in which every theatre is made up of a permanent salaried company of actors — managements and actors alike are keen to have plays with big casts, which keep as many as possible of the company's members engaged in performance. This, incidentally, is one of the main reasons why productions of Soviet plays are relatively rare in Great Britain, where — apart from a few big, subsidised companies — the opposite conditions prevail and production costs have to be kept as low as is compatible with decent artistic standards.

A Man with Connections shows Gelman as a master at constructing a two-hander — a unique challenge to an author's skills. Appalled but fascinated, we are drawn into a merciless duel between a pair of all-too-seasoned antagonists — a long-married couple — in which the moral and psychological advantage slithers from one partner to the other as the struggle sways this way and that. The tension slackens and then rises again as each contestant in turn pulls out stone after stone from the satchel of the past to sling at the other. One doesn't have to be a sovietologist to appreciate the play at this, its most basic level; in this respect it belongs in the same league as Albee's *Who's Afraid of Virginia Woolf?* But some clues to the specifics of the Soviet context can help us appreciate it to the full.

Gelman's ultimate target is the mechanism of the Soviet economy, with its dreadful inflexibility, clumsiness and inefficiency which, combined with a rigidly hierarchical 'command' system of management, regularly fails to produce the goods (significant exceptions to this are those branches of the economy that are geared to ultimately non-economic aims and are inherently susceptible to command-type management: the armaments industry and the space race). Being the kind of writer that he is, Gelman is not particularly interested in whether or not the Soviet industry produces enough missiles or concrete or machine-tools or nut and bolts: he is interested in people, and he has singled out an industrial manager as being a particularly glaring example of the — literally — inhuman pressures with which the system bears down upon the people working in it, people who, in fact, constitute a large portion of the total Soviet population and who are treated by that system (in Lenin's revealingly mechanistic phrase) like "little screws and cogwheels".

The all-powerful god of Soviet industry is The Plan, whose commands, like the Furies in pursuit of Orestes, threaten everyone who has the least degree of responsibility. In theory, since all production is ordained in advance by The Plan, the whole system should mesh together painlessly and efficiently, since factories A, B and C, for instance, are told to produce exactly the right number of components required by factories C, E and F in order that these, in turn, may fulfil *their* planned output targets — and so on down the line until the finished product reaches the consumer, whose wants are supposed to have been accurately predicted five years in advance by The Plan. In reality, this system has never worked properly, and it is the Soviet economy's decades of cumulative shortfall and failure which have produced the basically economic crisis that Gorbachov is — at last — tackling with his radical proposals.

The only means by which this lumbering, Heath Robinson mechanism manages to function at all, even with such inadequate results, is through the desperate efforts of managers at all levels, who deploy an astounding array of under-the-counter deals, 'old-boy' arrangements, barter, 'fixing', fudging, bribery and coercion. And because most of this has to be done on or beyond the fringes of legality (Soviet law prescribes very severe penalties of 'economic crimes', up to and including the death penalty), to be a manager in Soviet industry is one of the most stressful occupations in the world. It is only made tolerable by the often considerable chances open to them of feathering their own nests, and by the fact that because they are *all* in it, most managers are themselves too compromised to risk shopping their colleagues. Anyone who tries blowing the whistle is likely to get destroyed, too, in the ensuing crash. It is precisely this nerve-wracking kind of situation that has so eroded the human qualities and powers of judgement of Andrei Gladkov, the central character of Gelman's play, as to cause him to make the rash blunder which finally brings down Nemesis upon him as a man: it cripples his son for life and destroys his marriage. But it doesn't end his career: a skilled survivor in his particular world of distorted values, he 'manages' even this crisis so well that he actually gets promoted.

A MAN WITH
CONNECTIONS

The British premiere production of *A Man with Connections* was first staged at the Traverse Theatre, Edinburgh, on 4 August 1988 and subsequently at the Royal Court Theatre, London, on 6 January 1989.

The cast was as follows:

ANDREI GLADKOV	Bill Paterson
NATASHA GLADKOV	Marty Cruickshank

Directed by Jenny Killick
Designed by Dermot Hayes

The text printed here is the version used for this production and is somewhat shorter than the original Russian. A full translation – also by Stephen Mulrine – is printed in the volume *Stars in the Morning Sky*, an anthology of five Soviet plays introduced by Michael Glenny.

ACT ONE

*The action of the play begins with a prolonged impatient ringing at the
doorbell of the Gladkovs' apartment. The Gladkovs have a three-roomed
flat, but only one bedroom is visible on stage. The room is dark, now around
11 p.m. No one answers the door, and we hear more ringing – in short and
long bursts, now playful, now irritated. There is no response, and we hear a
key being turned in the lock.*

ANDREI'S VOICE *(from the hallway, with exaggerated affection).*
Natasha, sweetheart? *(Silence.)* Natalya, where are you?
Natalya, are you there?

There is no answer. ANDREI *comes in. He is short and thickset, 47
years old. Despite his bulk, and a certain puffiness, he is well set up
and stylishly dressed, wearing a fashionable raincoat, thrown open. He
carries a hat. He switches on the light – there is no one in the bedroom.
A little troubled, he rapidly checks out the other rooms. Finding no one
in the flat,* ANDREI *returns, and now begins to inspect the bedroom
more closely. The bedroom is in total disarray: in the middle of the
room, clearly not in its rightful place, stands a low, wide armchair;
wooden coathangers lie scattered across the floor.*

ANDREI *(to himself, gloomily).* Huh – a tip.

*He flings his hat and coat down on the divan, crosses to the telephone.
He takes a tiny notebook out of his jacket pocket, looks up a number.
He picks up the receiver – there is no dialling tone. He rattles the rest,
shakes the telephone, but it has obviously been unplugged. He picks up
the plug from the floor, pushes it into the telephone socket. He lifts the
receiver again, sits down on a chair, and dials the number.*

Hello? Men's Surgical? Yes, I'm enquiring about Alyosha
Gladkov, in Ward 3. This is his father – oh, hello, I didn't
recognise your voice. Yes, we'll be picking Alyosha up
tomorrow. How long has he been in? Um, let me think . . .
thirtieth of June, was the accident . . . that's um, just over a

month. Actually I'm looking for my wife. (*Jocularly.*) I've lost my spouse – she's not with Alyosha just now, is she? . . . I don't suppose she could've come in without your noticing? I mean, she's a pretty fast mover. Not possible? Would you do me a favour, please – ask Alyosha if his mother's been in today at all? Thank you, Sister. (*A pause.*) Yes, yes – I see. (*Looks at his watch.*) No, no, don't wake him up. Let him sleep. Right, thank you – sorry to trouble you – 'bye. (*Hangs up, dials another number from memory.*)

(*Coldly*). Hello, Vadim – it's Gladkov. Listen, I've just been down in your section an hour ago, and you haven't got that bloody girder up yet. OK, never mind the excuses – I won't be in the first half of tomorrow, I'll be there about two, and I want that girder in place by then, right? That's the first thing. Secondly – is my wife by any chance with you? You haven't seen her? Look, ask Olga, see if she has any idea where Natasha might be. (*A pause.*) Oh, hello, Olya . . . no, she's not here . . Well, she's not here now, when did she phone? Well, I don't know, maybe she wasn't phoning from home. Look, what are you so nippy about? Has Vadim been complaining again? I'm giving him a hard time? I'm giving *myself* a hard time, this job's behind schedule, he knows the position . . . Well, if it's not that . . . oh, come off it, Olga, I know damn well what it is! Hello? Hello? Shit!

Slams down the receiver, sits for a moment glowering, depressed. He removes his jacket, hangs it on the back of a chair, takes off his shirt and tie, and carefully spreads the shirt out on top of his jacket. He keeps his vest on, and lifts the phone again. He is in a better humour now, self-important.

Hello, Despatch? Gladkov here. How's that cement – are we unloading it yet or what? (*He picks up the telephone, and walks with it to the door, talking all the while.*) Mm – what about No 3 Pump – have they given us an operator? Well, I did ask. Look, chum, what do I need to do to get it into your skull? You get that concrete down there right away. Oh, and make a note in the day-book, I won't be in the first part of tomorrow, I'm going to the hospital to pick up the boy. So you can send the car for ten o'clock, not eight as usual . . .

ANDREI *passes from view into the bathroom. The telephone cord is very long, and it keeps unwinding until eventually it will extend no*

*further. We hear taps turned on in the bathroom. Suddenly, with a
sharp blow from inside, the doors of a roomy built-in wardrobe are
flung open.* ANDREI's *wife* NATASHA *crawls out, dishevelled and
dejected-looking, wearing a dressing gown which reaches to the floor.
She is 42. She seems distracted, her eyes glazed over, her breathing
irregular and agitated. She makes her way unsteadily to the armchair
and settles into it, tucking her legs underneath her. There is something
ominous about the way she sits, shivering, pressing herself into the
chairback. The water in the bathroom is turned off, and* ANDREI
*comes in again, stripped to the waist and washed, drying his neck with
a towel. He catches sight of* NATASHA *in the armchair.*

ANDREI (*startled*). Where have you been? (*At the sound of his voice*
NATASHA *shudders, and covers up her face.*) Eh? Natalya –
where did you spring from? (NATASHA *is silent.* ANDREI
notices the wardrobe doors, makes the connection, tuts disapprovingly.)
What have you been up to? Hiding in the wardrobe? (*No
response.*) Natasha? (NATASHA *looks up, seems on the point of
making some kind of spiteful or rancorous response, but suddenly goes
limp, drops her head again.*)

ANDREI (*gloomily*). Have you been drinking again? Have you
been drinking, I'm asking you? What are you playing at –
we're supposed to be picking Alyosha up at the hospital
tomorrow. How much have you had? Well, come on, how
many glasses?

    NATASHA *draws her head into her thin, bony shoulders – almost as
if she is trying to stop up her ears, so as not to hear* ANDREI's *voice.*

ANDREI (*bitterly*). So, OK, you've been drinking, terrific! We can
all get drunk together now. Alyosha can join in, make it a
threesome. Only we won't all fit in the wardrobe. So who's
going to do the driving, eh? Alyosha's no use now. We'll just
have to take the bus. Get rid of the car, I mean, what do we
want with a car? Will I turn on the shower? I'm asking you,
do you want a shower – bring you round a bit? (*He shakes her
by the shoulder.*) Natasha?

NATASHA (*shrilly*). Don't!

ANDREI (*taken aback*). Don't what? Don't turn on the shower?
Eh? Don't what? (*Looking at her back, sighs.*) My God Natalya,
the minute there's trouble you just go to pieces. I've been at
you for a month to snap out of it. Think of Alyosha. Crying

won't give him his hands back, you can't stick them on with tears. All right, our son has lost his hands – what are we going to do about it? There's no point in piling one tragedy on top of another . . . You know there was a phone call this morning, from the college? Wanting to know how he was getting on. I told them he'd be transferring to part-time. Have you decided yet which room he's having? It was you that was doing all the shouting that he couldn't stay in his old room. And why is his guitar still there? I thought we'd agreed – either give it to somebody or chuck it out. I think Alyosha should have this room – do you agree? (NATASHA *does not answer.*) Are you listening? Natasha? You're not even with us, are you? Anyway, while you've been otherwise engaged, I've been looking after Alyosha's interests. You know, it suddenly struck me – (*Taps his forehead.*) – this is a big town, there must be other people in the same boat. So anyway, I sent our chief mechanic along to the Welfare Office, and he turned up three – wrote down their addresses and went to see them. (ANDREI *sits beside her on a low stool.*) One's still quite a young chap, thirty-two, history graduate from Kiev, stays with his mother. The other two comrades are getting on a bit – war invalids. But they've got families, children – grandchildren. So it's perfectly normal, I mean, people go on *living.* Alyosha'll take a wee while to get settled, then we'll put him in touch with these chaps – maybe cheer him up. Also I got our mechanic to make notes on various gadgets they had. Like a foot-operated switch for the TV – so you can change channels. You just press it with your foot, like so – (*Demonstrates.*) Eh? And we'll try and get one of these push-button phones – the mechanic was saying they're really neat. You pick up a pencil in your teeth – beep-beep-beep-beep – (*Demonstrates.*) – and you've dialled your number, no problem. The receiver's mounted on a sort of vertical bracket – you just put your ear against it, and . . .

NATASHA (*shrieks*). You devil! Shut up! Shut up!

ANDREI. What? (*Outraged, gets up from the stool.*) Devil? Who's a devil? Eh? Well, thanks a bunch, Natasha – that's some word you've dug up. My God, you're good at dishing it out, but you don't see *yourself.* (*Goes onto the attack.*) What was the phone doing unplugged? I've been phoning you the whole day, like an idiot. Trying to let you know I'd be late in. There was a hold up at the site, we've three projects to wrap up by the first of the month. Of course, you won't be interested in my problems, you've found yourself a devil. *(Gives the coffee table with its unwashed cups a spiteful kick.)* Who've you been drinking with, eh? Who was it? Somebody just drop in? (NATASHA *does not answer.* ANDREI *continues, angrily.*) How do you want your shower, hot or cold? I'll run it hot to start with, but you finish off with a *cold* shower, right? A really stinging cold shower, that's what you need. Bring you to your senses.

He snatches up his coat and hat and goes out. Left alone, NATASHA *reaches into her dressing gown pocket for cigarettes and a lighter. She straightens herself up in the armchair, lights a cigarette.* ANDREI *comes in again, now bare-foot, wearing only his trunks.*

ANDREI *(cheerfully)*. Natasha, where's my dressing gown? It was hanging up in the bathroom. Have you seen it? (NATASHA *turns round sharply to face him, hatred in her eyes.* ANDREI *is disconcerted.*) My dressing gown, do you know where it is? Natasha, what's up with you? What are you staring at? (NATASHA *smiles contemptuously, her eyes ice-cold.* ANDREI *approaches and peers into her face.*) Listen, Natasha, *have* you been drinking? I think you're stone cold sober. *(Comes closer still.)* Right, then, breathe out. (NATASHA *shrinks into the corner of the armchair.*) Come on, let's smell your breath. Breathe out. *(He leans over her,* NATASHA *turns her face aside.)*

ANDREI *(coarsely)*. Come on, Natasha, bloody well breathe – *(Tries to come at her from the other side)*. Goddammit! (NATASHA *suddenly spits full force into his face, several times.* ANDREI *is thunderstruck.*) What the hell was that for? Eh? What was that for? *(He wipes his face with his hand.)* You're not drunk, Natasha, you haven't touched a drop . . . what's the matter with you? Natasha, this is *me*. What's up with you? What were you doing in there? *(Indicates the wardrobe.)* Have you been seeing things, Natasha? My God, that's all we need. Where's the phone? Where did I leave the phone?

ANDREI *remembers he took the telephone into the other room, hurries out.* NATASHA *gets up, has another couple of puffs and stubs her cigarette out on the ash tray. Then she crosses to the wall socket and pulls out the telephone plug, and stands with her back to the wall, concealing the socket.* ANDREI *rushes in, holding the telephone.*

ANDREI. Right, plug that phone in! I've just got through to
  Saratov – my mother's neighbour's gone next door to get
  her. I want to speak to my mother – plug that back in!
  (NATASHA *does not react.*) Plug that phone in right now!
  (NATASHA *refuses to budge, and* ANDREI *goes up very close to
  her, his manner now placatory.*) Natasha, my mother's there.
  She'll be worried. She'll be expecting me to phone back.
  She's an old woman, Natasha, she's not well. I'm phoning
  her now so's she'll make the eleven o'clock train and be here
  in the morning. We can't cope without her, Alyosha's
  helpless. I've got these projects to finish, I can't take time off.
  We'll do a quick trip in the morning, pick up Alyosha, I'll
  stay for an hour or so, then scoot. I mean, just don't count
  on me for the next couple of weeks – this is a crucial time for
  me, it really is. You can't imagine. And I'm sorry, Natasha,
  but you . . . That's why we need Mum. Look, I'm asking you
  to think about Alyosha. That's all that concerns us now,
  right? Just get that into your head – Alyosha, Alyosha, and
  that's it. OK? Natasha? Sweetheart?

NATASHA. Get dressed.

ANDREI. What was that?

NATASHA. Get dressed.

ANDREI. What for? What d'you mean dressed? Trousers?

NATASHA. Everything.

ANDREI. What's the point of getting dressed? Can't I phone as I
  am?

NATASHA. I'm not plugging this in.

ANDREI. All right, all right. (*Sets the telephone down on the floor. Goes
  out. Quickly comes back, wearing his vest, trousers, slippers.*)

NATASHA. That's not dressed. Fully dressed.

ANDREI. Listen, Natasha, my mother's waiting. Let me phone.
  Please? Just let me phone, then you can do what you like
  with me. Natasha! (*No response.*) Right, what do you mean,
  fully dressed? D'you want me to stick a hat on my head?

NATASHA. You heard me, everything.

ANDREI. Says who?

NATASHA. I do.

ANDREI. For God's sake! (*Picks his shirt up from the chairback, puts it on, stuffs his tie into his trouser pocket, picks up his jacket and puts it on.*) Now can I phone? Does that make you happy?

NATASHA. No. Coat. Shoes. Hat.

ANDREI. Natasha, that's enough! Plug that phone in, will you!

NATASHA. You heard what I said.

ANDREI. God Almighty! (*Goes out.*) I've no time for playing silly buggers, Natasha, I hope you know that!

NATASHA *meanwhile rushes to the wardrobe, opens the door, revealing a large suitcase. She drags it out and hauls it across to block the doorway, then returns to her position at the phone socket.* ANDREI *comes back, wearing his coat and hat, and his shoes, with the laces untied. He stumbles into the suitcase and capsizes it.*

ANDREI. What's that doing there? Some sort of bloody barricade? Right, plug that thing in now, this minute, and I'll phone for an ambulance! They'll give you an injection, to calm you down!

NATASHA. I'm calm enough, thank you.

ANDREI. Oh yeh, well, calm people don't sit inside wardrobes, Natasha. And they don't make their husbands wear hats to use the phone! You just bear in mind Alyosha'll have to stay in hospital until my mother gets here. And you're coming with me to the doctor's tomorrow, first thing.

NATASHA. Pick up your case . . . and get out.

ANDREI. What?

NATASHA. Your clothes are packed. Your dressing gown. And don't concern yourself about my health. I've never felt better in my life. Go on, take it and get out.

ANDREI. Who have you had here? What have they been telling you? I mean, everything was fine when I left this morning, the usual peck on the cheek, a wee wave – what's going on? What have you discovered? I can see it in that face of yours. Come on, what crime have I committed? You just remember how many times we've had this before. You've found me out, kicked up hell, divorce, the whole bit, then it's turned out there was nothing in it. Well, come on. What have you found out?

NATASHA. I've found out all I need to.

ANDREI. I'm asking you to tell me!

NATASHA. You better not ask. Because if I start to speak I'll kill you! That's why I hid, so I wouldn't kill you, do you understand?

ANDREI. Kill me? Oh yes, I see – I get the message now. It couldn't be anything else, could it. Somebody's told you that when Alyosha had his accident, that evening, I was at Sonia's house. Is that it? I'm asking you, Natasha, is that what you've found out? (NATASHA *is silent.*) What kind of idiot are you, eh? God Almighty, you're a fool! All right, so I *was* at her place. It was a house warming – her husband was there, her son was there – plus three other people out of the department! And by the time I got to the hospital you were in a terrible state – *that's* why I didn't tell you. I didn't want you thinking God knows what. As you're actually doing now. As you're *always* doing. That's why I said I was at a management meeting with Shchetinin. If you don't believe me you can ring up Sonia right now. God, you'll come back from the grave to keep an eye on me! There's no stopping you, is there – you've got a son lying in hospital, we're supposed to pick him up tomorrow, and you can't even find the time to tidy the place – you're too busy spying on me!

NATASHA (*interrupts him*). Just shut up about my son! You butcher!

ANDREI (*aghast*). What? What was that? Well, come on, repeat that!

NATASHA. Butcher!

ANDREI. Well, thank you very much, Natasha. I was a devil a minute ago, now I'm a butcher. So how come I'm a butcher, eh? Explain, please. Have you any idea what you're saying?

NATASHA (*interrupting, with increasing vehemence*). You knew! You *knew*!.

ANDREI. Knew what? What did I know?

NATASHA. Everything! You knew there was a power line there! You knew the crane could hit it! They told you! The supervisor even phoned up and warned you – he told you it was dangerous!

ANDREI (*interrupting*). Wait a minute, hold on –

NATASHA. Why did you send them?

ANDREI. Look, hold on –

NATASHA. Why did you send those men?

ANDREI. What *is* this? Are you accusing me? Alyosha's accident, is that what this is about? I thought this was –

NATASHA. You thought, you thought – you gave up thinking a long time ago! You go through life like a mechanical man – Shchetinin wound you up twenty years ago and you can't stop.

ANDREI. Look, Natasha, you can't just – I

NATASHA. You've destroyed Alyosha, that's what you've done!

ANDREI. For God's sake, Natasha, calm down! *Sit* down! I'll tell you what happened . . .

NATASHA. Don't bother, I don't want to hear it – just clear out!

ANDREI. Natasha –

NATASHA. Get out, I've told you – get . . . *out*! (*Pushing him towards the door.*)

ANDREI. Natasha, listen, listen – I'll tell you what happened! It was just the way things turned out – the end of the quarter, you know what *that* means. And I was twenty thousand down on the Plan, you know, to close the quarter. And that was the last day, the thirtieth of June. So I went to the Director. I went to Comrade Nikitin and asked him for an advance of twenty thousand right? I mean, his wife's my assistant, that's surely worth something! That's why I've got to keep in with Sonia, but you wouldn't appreciate that. Anyway, I asked him for twenty thousand and he said, get that road built by tomorrow morning and I'll sign. That's the road the accident happened on. But I mean, it's not his fault either, he wasn't to know . . . he just didn't want the Minister up to his neck in mud. I'd asked him for an advance and he saw his chance

to put pressure on *me*, right? There was about a half-day's
work in it, and I issued instructions to the section head to
organise a crane, bring up the slabs, and get it done. Then I
went back to the office. I'd no idea which brigade it would
be. I gave the order to the section boss, he relayed it to the
supervisor, the supervisor told the foreman, and the foreman
put a brigade on it. Alyosha's, as it turned out. I didn't even
know the exact spot. For God's sake, I've a whole construction site, five hundred acres! It was pure chance. I mean,
what can I do?

NATASHA. Get out.

ANDREI. Look, are you deaf or something? I've told you what
happened, it was coincidence. There's such a thing as
coincidence, you know, accidents *can* happen. You try to do
what's best. I had to find that twenty thousand, so the lads
wouldn't lose their bonus. I mean, you can't blame them,
but if they don't get paid their full whack they'll quit, and I
won't be able to replace them. And then the next quarter I'll
be deficient not just twenty thousand, but fifty thousand. You
thought you were acting for the best, getting Alyosha to do
his work experience with us. I was against it, but you were
adamant. If you hadn't insisted, Alyosha would have gone off
to some other town, and none of this would have happened.
But I'm not blaming you. I mean, what can you do? That's
just how it's turned out. You can't foresee these things.

NATASHA. Why didn't you cancel your order when the
supervisor phoned? He *told* you you weren't supposed to
work there, because of the safety regulations. Why didn't you
cancel? Eh? Didn't you have time to think? In too much of a
hurry to get to Sonia's?

ANDREI. There's no need to drag that in, Natasha. There's never
been anything between me and Sonia.

NATASHA. Oh, God – there's worse things in life than screwing
around. What's really frightening is people like you, brass-
necked, you don't give a damn about anything. Why didn't
you cancel that order?

ANDREI. I didn't give any order. I just said, if it's at all possible,
do it. And if it's too risky, forget it.

NATASHA. That's not what you said. People heard you, there were other people in the office. You said: I can't order you, but I'm asking you – please, please, *please* – it has to be done. You told him everybody's job depended on that road.

ANDREI. Well, that's right, it did.

NATASHA. What's right? What's *right*?!

ANDREI. I've *told* you – I was twenty thousand short, and Nikitin wouldn't give me an advance without that road. I had to ask him, so he asked me. It's standard practice, Natasha. If you remember, you couldn't get the books you wanted in the library last year, you and Olga – you were wanting some stuff by Trofimov –

NATASHA (*corrects him*). Trifonov.

ANDREI. Anyway, you came running to me – the book buyer had a burst pipe, could I do something about it? So I gave him a couple of plumbers, and *you* got your favourite bloody author. The plain fact is, there's a shortage of paper, and that's why there's no books. And I'm short of cement, that's why I'm down twenty thousand. That's why I sent those men – sent them to your book buyer, *and* out to that road! I thought they'd have a bit of sense, going under the wires, take it easy. As it turned out, it was an inexperienced crane-driver, a trainee. I mean, it just all came together!

NATASHA. And what would they have done, if you'd told the truth, eh? If you hadn't completed the Plan? Would they have shot you?

ANDREI. Look, for the tenth time . . .

NATASHA (*shouting*). I'm asking you – would they have shot you? I want an answer!

ANDREI. And I'm giving you an answer. If the crane-driver had been a bit more experienced it wouldn't have happened.

NATASHA. I want to know, Andrei – was your life at stake? If you'd just told them the truth for once, what could they do? Give you the sack, maybe? But they wouldn't do that, oh no – they couldn't get rid of you *that* easily, you're too well connected, you're like a bloody spider!

ANDREI. Natasha, I've got to work to the Plan, I have a
responsibility – managing CDC's like a sacred trust.

NATASHA. Then why did you send those men into a power line?

ANDREI (*agitated, shouting*). I didn't force them!
(*Out of the blue.*) Natasha, you haven't got something I could
take for a headache, have you?

NATASHA. No!

ANDREI. I've got a really splitting headache, you know?

NATASHA. Go to hell.

ANDREI. Natasha, I'll need to lie down for a couple of minutes,
my head's bursting. (*Moves towards the divan.*)

NATASHA. You didn't have a headache then, did you? The day
after – the *morning* after your own son lost his hands, when
you had to run back to your work! Straight from the hospital,
you just couldn't forget your twenty thousand, could you!

ANDREI. Natasha, there's no connection. Just stick to the point,
would you?

NATASHA. The point is that money had to be in on time, hadn't
it. You'd already sent word first thing, to Nikitin personally.
So you'd be able to include that money in the quarterly
figures – creative accountancy! You knew damn well Nikitin
would sign – I mean he could hardly refuse, after what had
happened. You made a use of your own misery, Andrei, just
so you could close your bloody quarter!

ANDREI. Natasha, there's no connection, Alyosha's one thing,
and the Plan's another. I don't get paid for being a husband
and father, you know!

NATASHA. When you told Sonia to go and speak to Nikitin, she
nearly fainted, did you know that?

ANDREI (*looks up*). What?

NATASHA. She was horrified.

ANDREI. What? What's Sonia got to do with it?

NATASHA. Sonia left here two hours ago. I got the whole story.
Your Director's wife has been here half the afternoon. I asked

her over to find out exactly where I stood. I was expecting to be told one thing, and I heard another. Far worse. (*Contemptuously.*) Oh, don't think you're in the clear there either. You know, when you rushed in from the hospital that morning, to rescue your damned Plan, she couldn't believe it, you left her practically in a state of collapse! She had to rush home, she didn't go to Nikitin. Somebody else got him to sign for your big fiddle. And when Nikitin found out, he told Sonia she wasn't to set foot in that menagerie again! So you've lost your assistant, she's leaving. You'll find her resignation on your desk tomorrow. D'you know we sat here crying, both of us? For the first time in my life I wanted to kill – physically wanted to kill someone. Can you understand that? Watching you getting out of your flash car, swinging your keys – full of yourself – striding along as if you hadn't a care in the world. I'm deadly serious, Andrei. I would have killed you right there and then. That frightened me. That's why I had to run into the wardrobe – out of fear. (*Shouts.*) I've never felt like that before, never! (*A pause, then suddenly.*) Is it true that you went down on your knees in Nikitin's office? When you were begging him for the twenty thousand?

ANDREI (*puzzled*). What?

NATASHA. You went down on your knees. His secretary saw you, she's telling everybody. How you opened the door and dropped straight onto your knees. (*Mimicking:*) 'Look how I've come to you, Comrade Nikitin, help me!' That's the truth, isn't it? You went down on your knees.

ANDREI (*glumly*). It was a joke.

NATASHA. A joke.

She crosses to the table, pulls out a drawer and flings a bottle of aspirin at him. It lands on the floor at ANDREI's *feet, and he picks it up.*

NATASHA (*suddenly*). And what's this money? (*She takes out a wad of ten-rouble notes.* ANDREI *turns to look at Natasha slowly.*) There's two hundred and fifty roubles here, Andrei. (*Shows him.*) Is it an advance on salary, or what?

ANDREI. It's my bonus money.

NATASHA. Bonus for what?

ANDREI. Well . . .

NATASHA. What bonus?

ANDREI. Well, it was for the quarter . . .

NATASHA. Which quarter? Last quarter? When you were twenty thousand short? When you went down on your knees? When Alyosha became a cripple?

ANDREI. Why are you asking? It was for . . .

NATASHA. Which quarter did you get the bonus for? That one? Was it? (ANDREI *is silent.*) Yes or no?

ANDREI. Yes! It was that one! (*A pause.* NATASHA *goes up to him, very close. When she speaks, her voice is filled with anguish.*)

NATASHA. That means that bonus money is for Alyosha's hands? That's right, isn't it, Andrei? That money is for your son's hands? (ANDREI *does not look up.*) And you took it. You accepted that money and brought it into this house.

ANDREI. Well, what else could I do? They gave me it.

NATASHA. Oh, of course, I mean what else *could* you do? If they gave you it. You're not going to look a gift horse in the mouth. And if they're demanding the *Plan*, you're not going to tell them you're short! (*Suddenly.*) Right, come here. (*She goes to the mirror.*)

ANDREI (*stupidly*). What for?

NATASHA. What d'you mean, what for? What did you do all *this* for? Go on – (*Pushes him bodily.*) – Go on, have a good look, see how well you've got on. Shchetinin's wee dog! Look at yourself. My God, somebody should paint you right now, and stick a caption on it: 'Portrait of a Manager that Closed his Quarter'. Put it on exhibition somewhere, so everybody can get a good look at you! (*A pause.*) Here! (*She thrusts the money at him.*) Take it! (ANDREI *takes the money.*) Tear it up! (ANDREI *lays the money on the table.*) What do you think I said? Tear it up! Listen you. I'll get on the phone this minute to every single one of your cronies' wives. I'll let them know what kind of dirty money their husbands earn. Tear it up.

ANDREI. All right, all right, I'll tear them up! (*Picks the money up from the table, tears the notes in half.*) Huh. Is there

anything else you want ripped up? Anything still left in one
piece? Just pass it across, I'll tear the lot up while I'm at it.

NATASHA. Oh, shut up. Now go and flush those down the toilet.
Go on.

NATASHA *watches as* ANDREI *gets up and trudges to the door.
He goes out, and we hear the toilet being flushed.* ANDREI *comes
back, sits on the edge of the divan.* NATASHA *stares intently at him
for a few seconds, then suddenly goes out. She returns almost
immediately, holding the torn notes in her hand.* ANDREI *looks
pained, hangs his head, stricken.* NATASHA *goes up to him,
scrutinises him very closely, a mocking, bitter smile.*

Still valid, are they? Still legal tender? My God, you're
pathetic. I suppose you were going to stick them together,
maybe buy Alyosha a wee gift – like a push-button phone!
Beep-beep-beep-beep-beep – there you are! (*She tears the
halved notes into shreds, flings them into* ANDREI's *face. The scraps
of paper flutter round the room.*) Right, come on, take yourself
off. Get out of this house. Go on.
ANDREI *rises reluctantly, moves towards the hall.*) The suitcase!

ANDREI (*pathetically, mutters*). I don't need it.

NATASHA. The suitcase, I said! (ANDREI *returns, picks up the
suitcase and again heads for the door.*) Wait! (ANDREI *pauses.*)
Leave the flat keys on the table! (ANDREI *returns once more,
takes the keys from his raincoat pocket, lays them on the table, lingers a
moment.*) What are you waiting for?

ANDREI *picks up his suitcase and leaves the flat. We hear him
slamming the outer door. There is a long silence,* NATASHA *stands
motionless in the centre of the room, her eyes closed. She is breathing
heavily, clearly disturbed. She takes a few steps to the divan and throws
herself on to it, face down. For a moment she lies there quite still,
motionless. Then she rises, crosses to the wardrobe and takes a
bathtowel out of a top drawer. She makes her way slowly out of the
bedroom. For a time the stage is empty, only the sound of running
water in the bathroom. Suddenly we hear a prolonged insistent ringing,
and simultaneous heavy thumping at the door.*

ANDREI'S VOICE (*from the landing*). Open up! Come on, open
up! Open this door! (*We hear him beating with his fists on the
door.*) Open up!

The hammering at the door grows louder – evidently ANDREI *is flinging his whole weight, and his suitcase, against it. Finally we hear a crack. He has broken open the door. Out of breath, enraged,* ANDREI *bursts into the bedroom. He flings down the suitcase and rushes out. We hear him battering at the bathroom door next, and the sound of the latch flying off as he breaks it open.*

ANDREI'S VOICE. Right, you bloody well come out of there! You can get washed later, just come out.

ANDREI *hauls her unceremoniously into the bedroom. She is naked, her bathrobe clinging to her damp body.* ANDREI *shoves her into the armchair.*

ANDREI (*shouting*). Who do you think you are – God? Mary the Mother of God? Eh? Just who do you think you are?

NATASHA (*looks at him with intense loathing*). Let me get washed. (*She makes to rise.*)

ANDREI. Sit down! (*Pushes her back.*) I don't give a damn if you never wash! What was it you called me? Brass-necked? Eh? (NATASHA *is weeping.* ANDREI *turns her head to face him.*) It was a different story twenty years ago, when you were in a communal flat with no bathroom – and of course, you couldn't *live* without a bathroom, not with your delicate upbringing. It was a different story then all right. Do you remember what you called me? Eh? A dumpling! A big soft lump! Well, that's where I started out, Natasha, with your blessing. The glory road from dumpling all the way up to brass-neck! Of course you were never like that, you were into everything, committed up to the hilt. Right from the word go. God Almighty. I'd hardly looked twice at her before she'd got me into bed! (NATASHA *rises abruptly,* ANDREI *pushes her back down.*) Sit down! And then later, of course, I see this is one smart student, definitely a whole lot smarter than me, and all mine, total commitment! My God, I was besotted! I gave you everything. I carried you around in my arms like a baby. Only I could never do anything right for you. You've always made me feel I had to keep at it, earn more, have more. You've always been at my back, driving me on. I mean, what else was that carry-on with Kuzmin but another way of getting at me, giving me a shove, eh? Sit down! . . . Of course there's no fancy men these days. Ever since I 'arrived', as you put it. That's now I'm earning three times

the salary, now we've a three-roomed apartment, a phone, a
car. You wanted all this as well, if you remember. Just cast
your mind back to eighteen years ago, when Shchetinin
called me into his office – the same office I now occupy.
'Listen, old chap,' he says, 'there's a party meeting tomorrow,
and there's somebody trying to bury me, so I'm asking you
to speak up, give me your support. Unless you want to sit on
your arse with the foremen forever.' That's what Shchetinin
said, and I came home that evening and told you the whole
story.
And, if you'd said no don't, I'd never have taken that step.
But all you said was – (*Mimics her.*) – 'Oh Andrei, sweetheart, I
don't know, it's up to you. I can't make up your mind for
you.' You weren't against it, you wanted it! Because you knew
damn well it was a chance to become Shchetinin's man. Sit
down! . . . I stayed awake the whole night, preparing that
speech – trying to get something together even *half* decent.
And all I could see was your eyes boring into my head. That
never-satisfied look. So I stood up, and made that speech! (*A
silence.*) And ten years ago, or what was it, twelve? . . . when it
all got too much, and I wanted to pack it in – did you
support me? Oh no – you clammed up. You just shrugged it
off. 'Don't do anything rash, Andrei, give it some more
thought.' You actually phoned Shchetinin – 'have a wee talk
with Andrei', you said, 'something's bothering him'. You
were terrified, that's the truth – shit-scared you were going to
lose it all, all the things you've got accustomed to. Plus a
cushy number at the library, drifting in and out whenever
you like, free as a bird. Only thanks to *your* job, I've got to
keep on that cretin – supposed to be a section head –
because he happens to be married to your boss, that bloody
Olga! D'you realise if I'd had a competent worker in his
place, possibly I wouldn't have needed to go down on my
knees for that twenty thousand? And Alyosha would still have
his hands! Well, do you still want to get washed? Or will you
pass, do you think?
(*A silence.*) You know, whatever I do out there, you're involved
here, Natasha. I'm sorry to say it, sweetheart, but I'm your
Five Year Plan. It's a business venture we have, not a family.
I mean, who do you think that money was for? Eh? Why am
I doing my brains in? I've got two suits, and that'll have to
do me until I retire! I've got a stomach ulcer, I can't even

enjoy a decent meal these days. And who is it all for? Eh?
Right, come on, stand up. (NATASHA *refuses to budge*.) Come
on, get up – I want to see your face. (*Tries to lift her forcibly.
NATASHA throws him off. ANDREI approaches again.*) You carry
on like a person with no past. Born again every morning.
Straight out the egg! Well, everything starts somewhere in this
life, Natasha. You say I shoved Alyosha under that power line
a month ago – I didn't mean to, God knows, it was an
accident – but you shoved me eighteen years ago, Natasha,
and that was *no* accident! And now you have the gall to
accuse me? To stand in judgement over me? Or sit, rather –
come one, get up out of there! Come on, stand up. (*He seizes
her by the shoulders, pulls her up.*)

NATASHA (*breaks free*). What do you want from me!

ANDREI. I want us to *live*, that's what. You've no right to fling
me out, after what's happened.

NATASHA. All right, I won't throw you out. You have a right to
stay, the law's on your side.

ANDREI. I'm glad *something's* on my side.

NATASHA. Oh, for God's sake! Do what you like! Just let me
finish washing, then I'll get dressed and *go*. Let me past.

ANDREI. No, I won't.

NATASHA. Andrei, I don't care, but I'm not living with you.

ANDREI. Yes, you are.

NATASHA. I'm not. You think that's the truth out now? You
wouldn't know the meaning of the word. You tell lies here,
you tell lies at work – you're an incorrigible liar, Andrei, but
you're not going to get away with it much longer. Your
'interpretation' of the facts, it's completely twisted – it's
pathetic!

ANDREI. I'm not twisting anything!

NATASHA. I didn't push you, you dragged yourself up. My God,
I'd enough trouble, trying to stay in one piece, with your
jealousy. You thought . . . you seemed to think that because I
went to bed with you so easily, it didn't mean anything to
me. You couldn't believe I might have done it for love, could

you? You still can't forgive me for that. But you don't want to
remember how I walked out on you, do you. You've
forgotten that.

ANDREI. I've forgotten nothing!

NATASHA. I was in love with Kuzmin, do you understand? I
thought I could have a new life. A different *kind* of life! Not
like this. And what did you do? My God, you practically
stood guard outside Kuzmin's flat. You even threatened to
take Alyosha away. That's why I went back to you. Yes. And I
hadn't been back three days before you started to cast up,
trying to humiliate me – even hit me. You did some terrible
things, Andrei, and I said nothing. You made out it was all
my fault. But it wasn't my fault – I just wanted to live like a
human being for once! And then something happened –
something very interesting. Actually the worst experience in
my whole life.

ANDREI. What are you talking about?

NATASHA. I'm talking about when Shchetinin was to be made
Group Manager, and you were in line for *his* job, running
CDC. And your promotion could depend on Kuzmin – he
was stepping up as well, you all were. But I knew nothing
about this, until Shchetinin suddenly phones me up and says
'Oh, Natalya, I'm sorry to bother you, but you know what's
happening here – do you think Kuzmin's likely to make
trouble?' And I said, 'What's it got to do with me? Why are
you asking me?' I said, 'Does Andrei know you're phoning
me about this?'

ANDREI. I didn't ask him to phone – I didn't!

NATASHA. And he said – 'He knows the general outline!'

ANDREI. That's a lie!

NATASHA. Just calm down. Anyway, you came home eventually,
and I said Shchetinin had phoned. I said, 'Maybe I've done
the wrong thing, but I phoned Kuzmin and he wasn't there.'
I was waiting for you to go berserk. I thought you'd half-kill
me. But no – all you said was, 'Oh, give it a rest, Natasha –
I'm fed up hearing about Kuzmin.' Fed up! For a whole year
I hadn't been allowed even to mention his *name* in this
house, under pain of death. Just the week previously, when

Alyosha needed medicine, and Kuzmin's mother could have got hold of it – Alyosha's lying burning up, and you wouldn't let me phone! Then suddenly it's, 'Oh, give it a rest, I'm fed up hearing about Kuzmin' – as if it was some old crow next door!

ANDREI. I don't remember this.

NATASHA. Really? And how about that same night, when you answered the phone, heard Kuzmin's voice, and hung up – do you remember that? And when he rang back, you said, 'You answer that, Natasha, I'm going to the loo.' You knew it was Kuzmin, and you went and sat in the bathroom! You didn't even hang yourself! And when I got dressed – at ten o'clock at night – and went out –

ANDREI. You told me you were going to Olga's. I remember that quite distinctly – you said you were going to Olga's. D'you mean to say you were with him?

NATASHA. Whether I was or wasn't, that's my business. You and Shchetinin needed help, and I gave it! You should have asked me then where I'd been. It was after one when I got home, you were pretending you were asleep –

ANDREI. I *was* asleep!

NATASHA. Oh, yes? And you cleared off out to work a bit smartly, so you wouldn't need to ask what time I'd come home at. Or did it just slip your mind?

ANDREI. I didn't force you.

NATASHA. Oh no, you didn't force me – you just didn't *stop* me! And you didn't force Alyosha, you just wanted that road –

ANDREI. That's two different things – you never stick to the point.

NATASHA. That *is* the point! There's no difference, it's the same thing. Why didn't you just speak to Kuzmin yourself? How about it, old boy? Don't you screw up my career, and I'll let you screw my wife! What stopped you? Eh? You haven't a shred of decency – what stopped you? (*Suddenly.*) Did you know it was Kuzmin on the phone? Answer me? Did you know it was Kuzmin? (ANDREI *is silent.*) Oh my God. All these years. All these years I've been telling myself you didn't hear him, you didn't know where I was going. I mean, it was so obvious, but I was afraid to believe it, I was afraid even to mention it, in case . . . (*A silence.*) I can't take this . . . I can't take any more. I wish I was dead.

ACT TWO

Fifteen to twenty minutes have passed, about the time of an act Interval.
The lights go up to reveal the Gladkovs' bedroom as before. ANDREI *is out*
of breath and dishevelled. NATASHA *is now wearing a skirt and sweater,*
and enters carrying a suitcase.

ANDREI. Look, hold on. OK, you're right. It's all true. You're
   right. But you've no idea what I've had to go through, to sink
   to that level. I'm serious, it's a horror story, Natasha. I'm
   scared of everything, the stupidest things. I keep waiting for
   something – that they'll sack me, that they're out to get me.
   I'm frightened to unplug the phone at nights, in case they're
   suddenly looking for me and I can't be reached. Something'll
   come up, and I won't be there to handle it. I daren't be
   absent, I've got to be there the whole time. Not a day goes
   by but there's something I could be sacked for. The fact is, in
   twenty years I haven't once – in any single year, quarter,
   month – not once have I completed the Plan straight. There's
   always some sort of fiddle going on, even if it's only petty.
   But if I play it by the book, and report a shortfall, I'll be out
   the door. Somebody's just got to want a new face, and I'll be
   finished. That's all it needs, Natasha. That's why I have to
   keep at it the whole time, diving about all over the shop – so
   nobody'll get any ideas. D'you want to know what I dream
   about at nights? *Who* I dream about? Shchetinin. I dream
   about Shchetinin. Shchetinin at work, Shchetinin on the
   phone, Shchetinin at home, Shchetinin in my dreams!
   There's not just *one* Shchetinin, there's thousands of them.
   When he's not in his office, he's inside my skull! He's got an
   armchair, a desk, a bed even – all in my head! D'you know
   the only time I'm happy? When Shchetinin's happy. When
   I've pulled off some cowboy stunt or other, for the Group,
   and carried the whole can myself – kept his name out of it.
   Then he's absolutely delighted. And I'm ecstatic, like a
   bloody idiot. You want to know how I see myself? Eh? I
   mean, you tell me often enough, I've no decency, no
   conscience. No feelings. But it's not true, Natasha – I have all
   these things – decency, conscience, feelings, the whole kit.
   But that's exactly what it is, a kit of parts. Whatever's

required, I'll dredge it up from somewhere. Mister Versatile, that's me. You're dead right, it's just a pose. Deep down, I really believe everybody's on the fiddle, and if they're not, well, they're just thick. And look at me, eh? 'Portrait of a Manager that Closed his Quarter.' And what about us? Eh?

NATASHA. Forget it!

ANDREI. Forget what? You can't do that, Natasha. All right, I did know, or at least I'd a good idea you were going to Kuzmin that night. But I said nothing. I was frightened to ask, same as you were, I didn't *want* to know. I just hoped I'd got it wrong, somehow.

NATASHA. Andrei, forget it!

ANDREI. How can I! I'm not a man, Natasha – I may look like one, but I'm not, I'm not human! You were right – I'll do anything to keep people sweet – things no human being would do, even with a gun at their head. But that's it, Finito, I'm finished. I'm through.

ANDREI *is pacing up and down the room, suddenly approaches* NATASHA, *addresses her matter-of-factly.*

I'll put the kettle on now, we'll have a cup of tea, get up a bit earlier in the morning.

NATASHA. What?

ANDREI. We're going to the hospital . . .

NATASHA. If you turn up at that hospital, I'll tell Alyosha, right in front of everybody – I'll tell him the whole story, how you've made him an invalid for life!

ANDREI. I'm past caring, Natasha. Tell him. I'll tell him myself. I'll do anything, to keep us all together. The way I see it, it'll be a different life from now on. But it's up to you Natasha, whatever you decide, whatever *you* want. From here on in, Natasha rules!

Without replying NATASHA *crosses quickly to the wardrobe.* ANDREI *bars her way.*

NATASHA. Let me past, till I get my things.

ANDREI. Natasha, no. I'm serious. What I'm saying now, is
you're in charge. If you want your mother to stay with us,
that's fine. I've always been against it, but now I'm saying she
can come and live with us. I'm tearing up the house rules. If
you want to have Olga here, you go ahead – invite the whole
crowd. You wanted a dog, you can have one. I'll even find a
wee dog for you, bring it home. I'll take it out for walks and
. . .

NATASHA. For God's sake!

ANDREI. I know, I know, I'm talking rubbish – but I want
everything to be how you want it. You go ahead and draw up
a . . . oh, I don't know, a list of conditions, under which you
agree to stay with me. And I'll ratify them, item by item –
you just tick them off as I . . .

NATASHA. Shut up! Shut up! You're disgusting! (*Mimics him.*)
'Item by item', 'ratify' – what kind of language is that?

ANDREI. I'm sorry. That's garbage. But I'm giving you my word,
Natasha, you can have whatever you want.

NATASHA. I want you out of here.

ANDREI. Natasha no.

NATASHA *turns and moves decisively towards the door.* ANDREI
catches her up, stops her.

Natasha, you're not leaving! Listen, listen – let's give it ten
days – give me a trial period of ten days, and if you're still
determined after that, then I'll go, I'll just disappear out of
your life. But you'll be satisfied, I *know* you will. Even before
the ten days is up. All right? Come on, say yes. Say yes and
that'll be it. And I'll put on the kettle. And you'll see. Come
on, say it. Nod your head. A wee smile? Natasha?

NATASHA *turns, crosses to the table, and takes out a cigarette.*
ANDREI *follows her.*

(*She lights up her cigarette.*) Is that it? Natasha'sweetheart. Yes?
You're lighting up a cigarette. Can I take that as a sign of
agreement? Right, I'll take that as a sign, and I'll put on the
kettle, OK? A cup of tea, right? Fine, I'll put on the kettle . . .

ANDREI *hurries out to the kitchen.* NATASHA *immediately stubs out her cigarette, opens the wardrobe, flings a few things into her travel bag, snatches her coat off a hanger and rushes to the door. In the doorway she collides with* ANDREI. ANDREI *enters.*

ANDREI. What's going on? I thought we'd agreed ten days! I've got the kettle on!

NATASHA. I'm leaving.

ANDREI. No! No! No! No! No! . . .

NATASHA. Oh, stop it, for God's sake! (ANDREI *is silenced.*) Take off your coat! (*He removes his coat and hat, flings them on the divan.*) Sit down! (*Indicates the armchair.* ANDREI *meekly complies, and* NATASHA *moves to confront him.*)

What's bothering you – that I'm leaving, and you'll be stuck with the flat? Andrei I can't stay here. I'm going to stay at Olga's mother's. She's at her sister's in Leningrad, for the whole summer. Olga's giving me the key. I can't bring Alyosha back to this, I hate this flat, and you along with it. I don't want you in the same –

ANDREI. Natasha. I've told you, I know how to sort this out now.

NATASHA. No, you don't. You can't fix it this time, like you fix everything else. I don't want to see you and Alyosha in the same room.

ANDREI. Natasha, I know what we have to *do*! It'll be all right!

NATASHA. There's nothing you *can* do.

ANDREI. There is.

NATASHA. There isn't!

ANDREI. Well, all right, just kill me. (*Shouts.*) Kill me! Either that or trust me. I know what to do.

NATASHA. For God's sake, what can you do, what can anybody do!

ANDREI. I'll quit work.

NATASHA (*pulls a face*). You what?

ANDREI. I'll quit the job, pack it in. I mean, that's at the root of it. Isn't it?

NATASHA. You'll never give it up!

ANDREI. Natasha, I'm just not cut out to be a manager. I don't know what it is, but I just can't be a boss, *and* a human being, I'm incapable. Maybe some people can, but I can't.

NATASHA. I don't trust you, Andrei. I asked you to quit a year ago.

ANDREI. I will this time!

NATASHA. No, you won't.

ANDREI. Yes, I will. I can do it Natasha. Besides, I've no option, have I. I can't carry on the way I've been doing, you've made that abundantly clear. I stand to lose you *and* Alyosha. And for what? I've already left him a . . . cripple. What else has to hit us before I come to my senses?

NATASHA. It was a different story when it happened, wasn't it! A different bloody story altogether!

ANDREI. That's right, it was. But that's it over now, finished. It's always like this with me – the pressure builds up and builds up, till the moment arrives and that's it – kaboom! Like an atom bomb. Do you know how an atom bomb works! (NATASHA *does not respond.*) You don't know how they make an atom bomb? Seriously? Well, to produce an atomic explosion you have to have a very precisely calculated amount of uranium, right? Critical mass, it's called. Anyway, they take this mass and divide it in two, and as long as the two halves are kept apart, it can't explode. But as soon as they remove the shield, and the two halves come together, that's it – goodbye, Hiroshima, farewell, Nagasaki!

ANDREI *suddenly falls onto his knees before* NATASHA.

ANDREI. Natasha – give us a kiss, eh? Come on, love, you'll see – everything'll be fine. Let's go to bed now . . . we'll get up a bit earlier in the morning, I'll give you a hand to tidy the place. OK? Will I make up the bed? (NATASHA *is silent.*) You wait and see, Natasha, there'll be big changes once I pack in this job. God's sakes, I don't want to dream about Shchetinin. I want to dream about the sea, or the sky – I want to dream about you, Natasha. I mean, was I put on this earth to be a manager? No way! And I'm not going to drop dead if I have to give it up. Damn right I'm not. You'll see, Natasha, we'll make something better of our lives. You know, it really pains me to see you drinking, Natasha – you shouldn't do it, love, please don't. Please, give it up, eh? Promise? OK? (NATASHA *is silent still*.) Will I make up the bed?

NATASHA (*quietly*). Where will you go?

ANDREI. What do you mean?

NATASHA. Where will you get a job? What as?

ANDREI. I'm not bothered. I'll find some nice, peaceful, ordinary job. Something human. I'll go into teaching.

NATASHA. To do what?

ANDREI. To lecture. In the Building College.

NATASHA. What, for a hundred and twenty roubles a month?

ANDREI. Natasha, sweetheart, people get by – we'll manage on that, it's not that desperate.

NATASHA. We'll have to look after Alyosha his whole life, have you thought about that? You know what I dreamt last night?

ANDREI. No, what?

NATASHA (*under strain*). I dreamt Alyosha was married, and his wife was throwing him out of the house. You were there, and we were trying to talk her round. She was . . . she was a dreadful person, a big fat woman, hard as nails, and she was shouting, 'I've been running after this cripple of yours for three years, the flat's mine, I've paid for it!' You said something to her, and she started bawling into the other room, 'Volodya, come and fling these people out!' And then this Volodya appeared – with *huge* hands, enormous, with a big moon face. This is my new husband, she says, I've been living with him for three months now. And then she turns to Alyosha. Go on, Alyosha, tell them, she says.

ANDREI. That's awful.

NATASHA. And this Volodya comes up to you, and starts shoving you out, punching you in the face –

ANDREI. Natasha. That's hellish!

NATASHA. And Alyosha was just standing in a corner the whole time, crying.

ANDREI. Natasha, love, it was only a dream.

NATASHA. It wasn't a dream! That's what's ahead of us! (*Tearfully, wiping her eyes.*) We've got to leave him something, we've got to save. You've made him a cripple, and now you're going off to lecture – on a hundred and twenty roubles? *A month.*

ANDREI. All right, love – look, I don't have to quit, it's not as if they want rid of me. Quite the reverse –

NATASHA. I'm not living with you if you *don't!*

ANDREI. OK, fine. I'll pack it in.

NATASHA. When?

ANDREI. Well, I don't know.

NATASHA. Can you do it tomorrow?

ANDREI. Tomorrow?

NATASHA. Hand in your resignation tomorrow.

ANDREI. Well, OK, if that's what you want. But I mean they won't just let me go at a day's notice. They'll have to find somebody to take my place.

NATASHA. No, they won't. I'll go with you to Shchetinin. I'll have a talk with him. And if I have to, I'll go to the district committee – I'm a wife and mother, I've got rights as well! OK, now you can phone.

ANDREI. Phone who?

NATASHA. Shchetinin. So he'll see us in the morning. We're not going for Alyosha, until you've got your release date. Now phone. (ANDREI *checks his watch.*) Phone.

ANDREI *goes to the telephone.*

ANDREI. What have I to say?

NATASHA. Get him to see us tomorrow. Tell him what it's about. Well, go on.

ANDREI. Right, right. (*Lifts the receiver, then suddenly.*) Oh, bloody hell! Shit! (*Slams the receiver down.*)

NATASHA (*alarmed*). What's up?

ANDREI. I forgot!

NATASHA. What?

ANDREI. I forgot! Something else happened today, I was going to tell you about it, and I forgot. I mean, when you jumped out of the wardrobe, it flew right out of my head.

NATASHA. So what was it?

ANDREI (*stalling*). Well, actually . . . it's a bit . . . well, to cut a long story short, I've been promoted.

NATASHA. What?

ANDREI. I've been appointed Group Manager.

NATASHA. You've been appointed what?

ANDREI. I've been made Group Manager . . . in place of Shchetinin.

NATASHA. They've made you Group Manager in place of Shchetinin?

ANDREI. That's right, Natasha – they've made me Group Manager in place of Shchetinin.

NATASHA. You?

ANDREI. Me.

NATASHA. They've suddenly made you Manager? That huge organisation? Three thousand men?

ANDREI. Oh don't worry, Natasha. I'm leaving – only not immediately, not tomorrow. I can't do that, there's –

NATASHA (*interrupts*). Why can't you do that?

ANDREI. Natasha, let me finish. You see, there's a whole chain – Shchetinin's being transferred to Head Office. I'm taking over from Shchetinin, one of the section heads takes over from me, somebody else takes his place, somebody else takes his, and so on, and so on. If I hand in my resignation now, that'll all fall apart. I'll be letting people down. That's why I'm asking you to change your mind, to wait a wee bit with the resignation. I'll accept the Group job, everybody'll move into place, and then I'll quit straight away. No problem. No unpleasantness.

NATASHA. No!

ANDREI. What d'you mean no?

NATASHA. I don't believe a single word of it! Why didn't you tell me this when you came in? You forgot, eh? Well, you just show me how you managed *that* – prove it!

ANDREI. All right, I didn't forget. I was going to tell you tomorrow, when you'd calmed down a bit. I mean, it really isn't my fault – the rotten bad luck and this promotion just happen to have coincided.

NATASHA. Coincided. Well, Alyosha's paid for that coincidence! It all worked out so nicely for you, didn't it? It wasn't just anybody that got hurt, it was your own son! And they felt sorry for you – poor Golubev, he's had to suffer. Only he *hasn't* suffered, he's positively bloody thriving on it! Now I know why you were grinning when you came home. Promotion! Victory!

ANDREI *crosses to pick up the phone, grim-faced.*

NATASHA. Who's that you're phoning now?

ANDREI. Shchetinin. I'm telling him to stuff his job, and I'll give him my resignation tomorrow. (*He starts dialling the number.*)

NATASHA. Put it down.

ANDREI *stops dialling, turns round to face her.*

Put the phone down. (*He replaces the receiver.*) Switch off the kettle!

ANDREI. What?

NATASHA. The kettle, switch it off.

ANDREI *switches off the kettle.* NATASHA *lights up a cigarette.* ANDREI *makes some tea. He gives one glass to* NATASHA. *Silence. Sipping tea.*

NATASHA (*after a pause*). I suppose I should congratulate you, on your promotion! (ANDREI *does not respond.*) Well, what are we going to do?

ANDREI. Just keep going. Stay alive. Look I'm sorry about all this, Natasha, I really am. Why don't we just talk about it eh?

I mean, essentially why is it you want me to quit? You want
it, and I want it – why? Because as it is it's nerve-racking –
my head's nipping with it the whole time. Eh? But it doesn't
have to be like that, it could all be different. I mean, look at
what's happening now. Shchetinin'll be leaving. That means I
won't have him breathing down my neck any longer – all that
pressure. Group Manager's not like running CDC – it carries
a lot of clout, you know, you're practically a free agent. I
mean, there's one level of activity, where you're dependent
on circumstances, like managing CDC, and then there's
another level, where you *create* those circumstances. Group
Manager's on *that* level, it's like stepping out into the strategic
heights.

NATASHA. Oh, for God's sake.

ANDREI. Natasha, I am forty-five years of age and for the first
time I've got an opportunity to really *do* something! And do
it *my* way. I won't get an opportunity like this again, it just
won't happen. D'you understand? All right, so it's come up
at the wrong time, it's not exactly the happiest moment of
my life. It's actually the bloody worst imaginable. But if I *am*
going to carry on living, what am I supposed to do – bury
myself? I want to give it a try, Natasha. I've got ideas, and
know-how – I can turn this job around. I'll pick out some
really bright people. I mean, I know where to find them –
first-rate qualified people, out in the cold and I'll bring them
in, give them good jobs, put together a team. We'll have a
real think-tank, Natasha.

NATASHA. And what will you do with the people you've got
now?

ANDREI. Get shot of them! We're needing to turf half of them
out anyway, and I'm just the man to do it!

NATASHA. Oh yes? And how are you going to do that? They're
all Shchetinin's people. The first sniff of trouble, they'll be on
the phone to Shchetinin and he'll tell you to lay off. And you
won't go against Shchetinin.

ANDREI. Well, that's life, Natasha. I've been Shchetinin's man
long enough. OK, so there'll be trouble. But I've kept my
head down long enough. But I just want to give it a shot, eh?

Now I'm not going to take on more than I can realistically handle, like Shchetinin. That's the cause of this whole mess: he promised them too much and it all started to hit the fan. Well, I won't do that – I'll tell them straight, these are the resources you've given me, this is what I can build, and that's it. That's your lot. And if they don't like it, then sod them, I'm off.

NATASHA. How are you going to walk in as somebody else – plastic surgery?

ANDREI. I've thought about that as well, Natasha, I really have. Maybe it's a terrible thing to say, but that's exactly where Alyosha'll be a help. Everybody knows why my son lost his hands. I think that gives me the right, as a human being, to just walk in and tell them. That's it. The game's up. It definitely wouldn't have been easy a month ago, but I've got the *right* to change things now. Don't think I don't know what's ahead of me. This big clear-out's going to need God only knows what sort of strength and persistence. And the kind of good health I frankly don't enjoy. You don't know the full story. The ulcer's one thing, that's OK, it comes and goes. But this last while back, I've been tiring very quickly . . . In the middle of the day I've been asking my secretary not to let anybody in, and getting the head down on the desk, for a half-hour or so. Otherwise I just can't work . . .

NATASHA. That's because you haven't had a break two years on the trot. How many times have I told you, you need a rest!

ANDREI *smiles affectionately, draws* NATASHA *to him, a chaste kiss.*

ANDREI. Never mind, love, I'll survive. You've no idea how grateful I am, Natasha. I know how hard it is for you to accept what's happened – believe me, I know. (*Kisses her warmly.*) Natasha, I swear I'll do whatever you want, I promise – I love you, Natasha – I'll do everything I possibly can, you'll see –

NATASHA. Andrei, if there's going to be any more lies . . . the way it's been – I just couldn't . . .

ANDREI. I know.

NATASHA. I just couldn't take any more lying – physically I couldn't. The slightest . . .

ANDREI. I know . . .

NATASHA. You've got to promise me, if it doesn't work out, you'll quit right away?

ANDREI. Of course.

NATASHA. And you can change, Andrei, you know that . . . if you really want to.

ANDREI. I can. And I will.

NATASHA. I sometimes wake up in the middle of the night and look at you. You look nice when you're asleep, when your face is relaxed – it's sort of friendly and open, like a wee boy. *My* wee boy. I look at you, and I start to cry – I don't know, it's just . . . Andrei, I'll really do something to myself this time, if you start . . .

ANDREI. Natasha, love, don't – I know, I know.

NATASHA. I wasn't going to tell you . . . but when you came home tonight, and you were on the phone – I was in there *(Indicates the wardrobe.)* and this terrible feeling came over me. It was all just too much, you sounded so obnoxious. And then what Sonia had told me . . . And the darkness . . . I was searching around for a belt or something. I'd found a place I could hook it onto . . .

ANDREI *(starts up)*. You what?

NATASHA. It's the truth . . . if you'd stayed there five more minutes, it would have been all over. You just left the room, and I fell out onto the floor. Like out of a grave.

ANDREI. Natasha, for God's sake, don't! Don't say any more – we'll get through this, we will! We'll still dance at Alyosha's wedding – *and* we'll babysit for him when the grandchildren arrive! We'll get this business up and running, Natasha, we'll *build* something in this town, eh? What d'you say? Natasha, honey, come on, Natasha, sweetheart – *(Kisses and cuddles her.)* I love you, Natasha, you know I do . . .

NATASHA *(tearfully)*. Oh, Andrei, Andrei – will you do something for me?

ANDREI. Of course I will, pet – what is it?

NATASHA. I mean if you did agree Andrei, then I really would believe you were serious . . . Andrei, I want to leave the library. So you can take me on at your place. I want to work alongside you, Andrei. To be involved, so I'll understand.

ANDREI. Yes, sure, love – no problem. I'll give it some thought. (*Kisses her.*)

NATASHA. Do you mean that? Really?

ANDREI. Why not?

NATASHA. I deliberately didn't get involved before, I didn't want to . . . I mean, that was *my* fault, and I'm sorry. But if I'm going to live with you, then we have to share everything. I couldn't stand that Shchetinin, but if there's going to be other people now, then I would have them here, put on a bit of a show for them – you could all get together here, discuss things . . . and I'd know everything that was going on. Please, Andrei, I really mean it, I want you to find me a job with the company. If you do that, then I definitely *do* think we could make a go of it. Will you do that? Andrei?

ANDREI. Mm, yes – Natasha, love, I'm just not sure what you could do in our set-up.

NATASHA. It doesn't matter. You have a records office, I could do that – any sort of paper work.

ANDREI. Mm. To tell you the honest truth, Natasha, it's a wee bit inconvenient.

NATASHA. Why is it inconvenient?

ANDREI. Well, I mean . . . I mean, how will it look if the new Group Manager arrives and the first thing he does is to set up his lady wife? It's a bit off, you know?

NATASHA. So what are you saying, Andrei? That you haven't understood? That you don't agree to it?

ANDREI. No, no, love, I understand. And I *do* agree. I'm all for it. Only not right away, OK? Give it time. I mean, if I bring you into the office on day one, it might be misinterpreted. It could actually interfere with what I'm trying to do, you know? We'll definitely do it, but we'll need to wait a wee while. OK? (*Kisses her.*) And you'll be able to help me at home meanwhile . . . I'll tell you everything. Every last detail, all right?

NATASHA. Andrei, it's got to be done *now* . . . right from the start. It's crucial, Andrei.

ANDREI. Natasha, honey, you just don't know what the public are like. I promise you, it *will* happen. Only not right away. I can't just assemble everybody and explain why I'm taking you on . . .

NATASHA. That's all right – if they want an explanation, I'll give them one. If necessary I can tell them why we've decided to –

ANDREI. God's sakes, Natasha, you're not serious! We *can't* do it, they won't buy it.

NATASHA. Is that the only reason?

ANDREI. Of course it is. What other reason could there be?

NATASHA. And when do you have to take over?

ANDREI. Well, there's no hurry. I should think I'll be at CDC for another six to eight weeks.

NATASHA. Well, that's fine!

ANDREI (*guardedly*). What d'you mean, that's fine?

NATASHA. Because Shchetinin can give me the job. Now, while *he's* still in charge. Shchetinin'll take me on, and when you arrive I'll already be there, nothing to do with you! (NATASHA *is overjoyed.*) A brainwave. (NATASHA *presents her cheek for* ANDREI *to kiss.* ANDREI *is dumbstruck.*) So that's it, then, I'll give in my notice to Olga tomorrow, and go and see Shchetinin. In fact, I'll ring him up right now and arrange it! Oh Andrei, it'll be so nice working together. And I know how to behave, you needn't worry . . . I won't come to work in your car.

NATASHA *crosses delightedly to the phone, lifts the receiver.*

ANDREI. Natasha, hold on.

NATASHA. What for? It's a fantastic idea, a stroke of genius. Who knows, you're maybe just about to acquire the most valuable member of your think-tank! You can put me in charge of public relations! (*Begins dialling the number.*) I'll congratulate old Shchetinin on his promotion first, and fix a time.

ANDREI. Natasha.

She carries on dialling the number regardless. ANDREI *crosses to the table, clicks off the rest.*

It's too late. They'll be asleep.

NATASHA. So what? He's not slow to phone you up at two and three in the morning – why shouldn't I phone him at half twelve? I'm sure he'll be delighted. Andrei, take your hand off the phone. Come on, love, move your hand.

ANDREI *does so, and* NATASHA *dials again. This time, however, he crosses to unplug the cord at the wall, and the line goes dead.*

ANDREI *(coldly)*. You're phoning nobody, Natasha. I'm not having you working beside me.

NATASHA. What?

ANDREI. It's just not on.

NATASHA. Why not?

ANDREI. It just isn't! I mean, what's the point? I don't need help at work. You can help me here. But not there.

NATASHA. Huh! *(Disgusted.)* My God. Is that your last word?

ANDREI. Yes.

NATASHA *(pathetically, confused)*. Andrei . . . I wanted it for us . . . for your sake. I wanted us to be together . . .

ANDREI. I'm sorry, Natasha, but you're talking rubbish.

NATASHA. So that's it, then?

ANDREI. Yeh, end of story.

NATASHA. And what about the promise you made, to do what I want?

ANDREI. Yes, well, *except* that. And you needn't think there's any funny business going on –

NATASHA. I don't think that, Andrei, it's *worse* than that! Keep off. Give you and Shchetinin a completely free hand? So you can electrocute people!

ANDREI. I damn well certainly don't need *you* checking up on me! There's enough folk doing that! Oh, no, maybe I got slightly confused, it's been like a madhouse. But that's it over. What's yours is yours, sweetheart, and what's mine's my own!

NATASHA. Oh, of course, that's typical – what's yours is yours, so far and no further. A madhouse? That's right, anything the least bit human *is* mad, as far as you're concerned. You'll end up putting me away in an asylum!

ANDREI. Oh, leave off, Natasha.

NATASHA. Oh, I'll leave, don't you worry.

ANDREI. I know damn well what you're after. You think you've got me by the throat? Well, you just remember, Natasha, who's got the brass neck.

NATASHA *turns pale, anguished, gasping for breath.*

NATASHA. God Almighty! I don't believe this . . . it's not possible . . . What am I doing here? Why am I still here? It's a judgement on me, I'll pay for this! One of these days I'll be judged for it, that I stayed married to you for twenty years! Nobody forced me, nobody made me do it – (*She picks up her coat and makes her way to the door.*)

ANDREI. Just stay there! (NATASHA *stops.*)
Turn round. Oh, don't worry, I'm not stopping you, you can go. But first let's get a few things straight. If it hadn't been Alyosha that suffered, but some other kid, you wouldn't have turned a hair! You'd have been tearing round the management trying to rescue me – you'd have run to your precious bloody Kuzmin. And rightly so! That's how it should be. You're supposed to be my wife, then *be* a wife. It's Olga that's put you up to this. She's actually said it to my face, I remember distinctly – 'You know, Andrei, Natalya should never have married you – her kind of man would despise people like you!' Bloody cow! Well, you go to her. Only you just remember, you're going of your own accord. Go on, go. And I'm staying put, right here. In my own place. I'm not just a husband. I'm an engineer, a manager, in charge of hundreds of men – huge resources. I'm a builder, for God's sakes, not a bloody librarian! It's people like me that have to carry the whole show on our backs!

NATASHA. Carry it where?

ANDREI. Wherever! But if you leave me, now, Natasha, you're on your own. I'm warning you, you step over that door and there's no way back! I let you back in once before, I'm not doing it a second time. You walk into that lift, press the down button, and that's it – as far as I'm concerned you're down and out forever. Now, beat it!

Turns sharply on his heel, and sits in the armchair, his back to the door. After a moment's hesitation, NATASHA *exits.* ANDREI *jumps up.*

ANDREI. Natasha, come back! (*He runs out into the hall.*) Come back here! Natasha, for God's sakes! (*Re-enters, stands in the middle of the room.*) Bloody hell! Shit! (*He flings open the verandah door, exits, and begins shouting from the verandah down to the street below.*) Natasha, come back here! There's no need for this! Natasha! Bloody bitch! (*Re-enters.*) Shit!

He crosses to the telephone, breathing heavily. He dials a number.

ANDREI. Hello, Despatch? Gladkov here. What took you so long? Oh save it! How's that concrete, is it in the pump yet? How many cubic metres? Yes, well you just remember, I'll be checking it in the morning. Oh, and by the way, I asked for the car at ten o'clock tomorrow, scrub that. Have it outside here at eight. The usual. (*Slams down the receiver. The phone instantly starts ringing, he picks it up again.*)

ANDREI (*gloomily*). Hello?

ALYOSHA'S VOICE. Dad?

ANDREI. Alyosha?

ALYOSHA'S VOICE. Did I wake you up, Dad?

ANDREI. No, no. What's up, son? Is there something you want? You know it's after one o'clock? I phoned earlier . . . they said you were asleep . . . what's wrong, are you OK?

ALYOSHA'S VOICE. No, I woke up again – I've been trying to get through for a wee while.

ANDREI. Yeh – we've been pretty busy. Listen son, I'm glad you phoned. Is there something up? I could drive over right now, no problem.

ALYOSHA'S VOICE. No, no, that's OK, Dad. I just felt kind of frightened, you know? And then I heard your voice, and everything was all right again. Is Mum asleep?

ANDREI. Your mum? Yes, she's asleep.

ALYOSHA'S VOICE. What time will you be coming for me tomorrow?

ANDREI. Tomorrow? Before lunchtime. We'll be there before lunch.

ALYOSHA'S VOICE. Am I keeping you out of bed, Dad?

ANDREI. No, don't be daft – I could chat away to you the whole night.

ALYOSHA'S VOICE. No, that's OK. I'll get back to sleep. Dad . . . everything's going to be all right, isn't it? Dad?

ANDREI. Yes, sure. Just you put it out of your mind.

ALYOSHA'S VOICE. Goodnight, Dad.

ANDREI. Goodnight, son . . .

> ANDREI *lowers his hand, holding the receiver, and we hear* ALYOSHA'S VOICE *continuing at the other end, trying to summon assistance to replace his receiver.*

ALYOSHA'S VOICE. Nurse? Nurse, will you help me, please? Nurse, I can't put the phone back, will you help me, please? . . .

> ANDREI *remains motionless, still holding the receiver. His eyes are glazed, a distracted look, off in another world somewhere, while the Line Open tone is heard, growing louder and more insistent, like an alarm signal.*

The End